A DAY WITH A GARBAGE COLLECTOR

by Avery Toolen
illustrated by Dean Gray

GRASSHOPPER

Tools for Parents & Teachers

Grasshopper Books enhance imagination and introduce the earliest readers to fiction with fun storylines and illustrations. The easy-to-read text supports early reading experiences with repetitive sentence patterns and sight words.

Before Reading

- Discuss the cover illustration. What do they see?

- Look at the picture glossary together. Discuss the words.

Read the Book

- Read the book to the child, or have him or her read independently.

- "Walk" through the book and look at the illustrations. Who are the main characters? What is happening in the story?

After Reading

- Prompt the child to think more. Ask: Would you like to be a garbage collector? Why or why not?

Grasshopper Books are published by Jump!
5357 Penn Avenue South
Minneapolis, MN 55419
www.jumplibrary.com

Library of Congress Cataloging-in-Publication Data

Names: Toolen, Avery, author. | Gray, Dean, illustrator.
Title: A day with a garbage collector / by Avery Toolen; illustrated by Dean Gray.
Description: Minneapolis, MN: Jump!, Inc., 2022.
Series: Meet the community helpers!
Includes index.
Audience: Ages 5-8.
Identifiers: LCCN 2021034099 (print)
LCCN 2021034100 (ebook)
ISBN 9781636903286 (hardcover)
ISBN 9781636903293 (paperback)
ISBN 9781636903309 (ebook)
Subjects: LCSH: Readers (Primary)
Sanitation workers—Juvenile fiction.
LCGFT: Readers (Publications)
Classification: LCC PE1119.2 .T6634 2022 (print)
LCC PE1119.2 (ebook)
DDC 428.6/2—dc23
LC record available at https://lccn.loc.gov/2021034099
LC ebook record available at https://lccn.loc.gov/2021034100

Editor: Eliza Leahy
Direction and Layout: Anna Peterson
Illustrator: Dean Gray

Printed in the United States of America at Corporate Graphics in North Mankato, Minnesota.

Table of Contents

The Garbage Route 4

Quiz Time! 22

Parts of a Garbage Truck 22

Picture Glossary 23

Index 24

To Learn More 24

The Garbage Route

Before the sun comes up, garbage collectors meet at the garage.

Tom and Tammy share a route.

They share a truck, too!

They make sure everything works.

They check the lights.

They check the lift.

lift lever

Tammy drives the truck.

Tom sits in the passenger seat.

Their route takes them
around the neighborhood.

They stop at the first house.

Tom gets out.

His vest has reflectors.

Drivers can see him
in the dark.

reflector

He loads each garbage bin.

Gloves protect his hands.

Boots protect his feet.

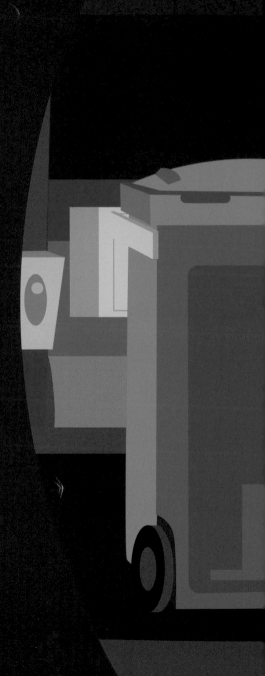

garbage bin

13

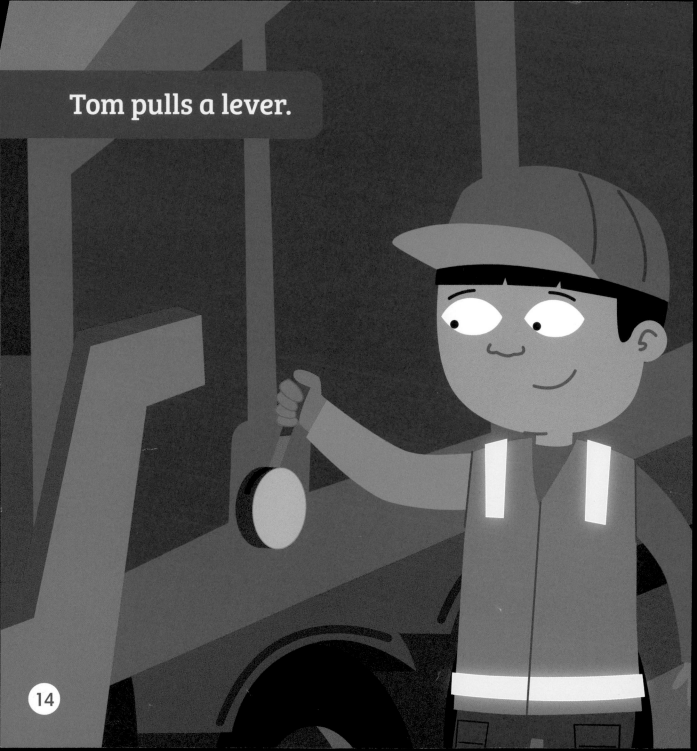

Tom pulls a lever.

14

A compactor crushes the trash.

This makes room for more.

compactor

Tom and Tammy visit all the homes on their route.

Then they go to the dump.

This is where garbage trucks dump trash.

Tom and Tammy go
back to the garage.

They put gas in the truck.

It is ready for
tomorrow's route!

Quiz Time!

What happens when Tom pulls the lever on the garbage truck?

A. the horn beeps   B. the lights turn on
C. the engine starts   D. the lift dumps the bin

Parts of a Garbage Truck

Take a look at the parts of a garbage truck!

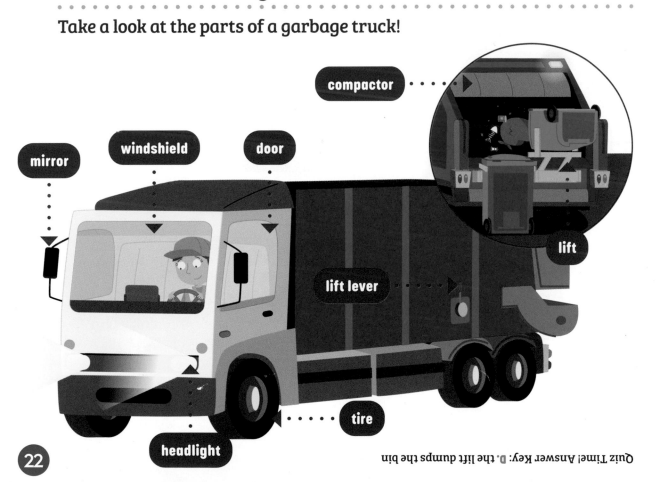

compactor

mirror

windshield

door

lift

lift lever

tire

headlight

Picture Glossary

compactor
A device that crushes and compacts trash to take up less space.

lever
A bar or handle used to work or control a machine.

lift
A device used to lift or raise something.

protect
To guard or keep something safe from harm.

reflectors
Shiny surfaces that cause light to bounce back.

route
The path that someone or something regularly travels along.

Index

boots 12

compactor 16

crushes 16

drives 8

dump 18

garage 4, 20

garbage bin 12, 15

gas 20

gloves 12

lever 14

lift 6, 15

lights 6

route 5, 9, 18, 20

trash 15, 16, 18

truck 5, 8, 15, 18, 20

vest 10

To Learn More

Finding more information is as easy as 1, 2, 3.

❶ Go to www.factsurfer.com

❷ Enter "**adaywithagarbagecollector**" into the search box.

❸ Choose your book to see a list of websites.